America's Seashores

Guide to Plants and Animals

Marianne D. Wallace

Fulcrum Publishing
Golden, Colorado

Cordgrass

Great
blue heron

Oysters

Atlantic croaker

Fiddler crab

Clam

MUDFLAT—HIGH TIDE

To Donald Page, my biology teacher at Inglewood High School, Inglewood, California. Mr. Page loaned me his very own copy of the book *Between Pacific Tides* to help me with my science project. He trusted me and supported my interest in marine life. I have never forgotten that.

Plants and animals shown on the front cover (clockwise from upper right): **Brown pelican, cormorant, harbor seal, oystercatcher, knotted rockweed, purple sea urchin, giant green anemone, ochre sea star, mussels, herring gull (on barnacles), beach pea, beach grass.**

Line of shells in text box (left to right): **Scallop, slipper shell, moon snail, coquina clam.**

Plants and animals shown on the back cover (clockwise from upper right): **Tern, sea oats, seaside goldenrod, eelgrass, beach morning glory, rock crab, oysters, raccoon tracks, red mangrove, snowy egret, great blue heron.**

Text and illustrations copyright © 2005 Marianne D. Wallace

Library of Congress Cataloging-in-Publication Data

Wallace, Marianne D.
America's seashores : guide to plants and animals / Marianne D. Wallace.
p. cm.
Includes index.
ISBN 1-55591-483-7
1. Seashore plants—Juvenile literature. 2. Seashore animals—Juvenile literature. I. Title.
QH95.7.W35 2005
578.769'9—dc22
2004030231

Fulcrum Publishing
16100 Table Mountain Parkway, Suite 300
Golden, Colorado 80403 USA
(800) 992-2908 • (303) 722-1623
www.fulcrum-books.com

Printed in the United States of America

0 9 8 7 6 5 4 3 2 1

Editorial: Katie L. Raymond,
Haley Groce
Design: Ann W. Douden, Patty Maher
Cover image: Marianne D. Wallace

Pickleweed or Glasswort

Table of Contents

Introduction to Seashore Life 4

North American Seashores 7

    North Atlantic Coast 11

    South Atlantic Coast 15

    Gulf Coast 19

    South Pacific Coast 23

    North Pacific Coast 27

    Arctic Coast .31

Common Plants and Animals 34

    Crabs and Other Arthropods 36

    Seashells, Sea Stars, and Sea Urchins 37

    Birds 38

    Mammals and Fish 39

    Anemones, Worms, and Other Soft Creatures 40

    Wildflowers .41

    Seaweeds, Kelp, and Other Algae 42

    Grasses and Grasslike Plants 43

Animal Tracks and Signs 44

Glossary 45

Resources 45

Common and Scientific Names with Index 46

MUDFLAT—LOW TIDE

Cordgrass

Oysters

Dowitcher

Clam

Fiddler crab

Introduction to Seashore Life

Pretend you are a **shore crab**. You live on a rocky beach along the ocean. Most of the time you are underwater. But every few hours the water starts to go away and waves crash against the rocks around you. You have to hide among the **seaweeds** or inside cracks in the rocks just to keep from being swept away. Then the water is all gone and the sun is shining. Your body is not designed to stay out of water very long so you must try to stay cool and wet until the water returns. Soon the crashing waves are back, the water level rises, and you are underwater once more.

This is what life is like for many **seashore** animals, whether they live on beaches of rock, sand, or gravel. In most parts of the world water levels in the ocean move up and down one or two times a day. These movements are called **tides** and are caused when the sun and moon's gravity pulls at the oceans on the Earth. Sometimes the change between the highest water level, or **high tide**, and the lowest water level, or **low tide**, is 1 to 2 feet (0.3 to 0.6 m) or less. But in other places the change can be much bigger. The world's greatest difference in tides—up to 53 feet (16.2 m) between high tide and low tide—occurs at the Bay of Fundy in Nova Scotia, Canada.

Map of Earth
The Earth has 220,720 miles (356,000 km) of coastline.

Animals that live in the area, or **zone**, between the high and low tides have found ways to survive. Some, such as the crab, hide in a rock crack or underneath something that will protect them from the waves and dry air. Animals such as **barnacles** and **mussels** either can't move or move too slowly to hide this way, so they close up tight and count on their hard shells to protect them. Other animals manage to remain underwater during low tide by staying in small pools on the rocky shore, called **tide pools**. These tide pools stay filled with water when the tide goes down. Lots of animals can be found here. Look for **hermit crabs**, **sea urchins**, **anemones**, and tiny fish called **blennies**.

Some of the most common things you'll see along the ocean's edge as the tide goes down are **algae**. They look like plants covering the rocks. Although there are many

Blenny

shapes, colors, and sizes, most of the algae you'll find belong to one of three groups: **green algae**, such as **sea lettuce**; **brown algae**, such as **rockweed**; and **red algae**, such as **Irish moss**.

Another type of area along the ocean shore is called an **estuary**. This is where rivers flow into the sea creating **deltas** and **bays**. This mix of freshwater from the river and salt water from the sea is called **brackish water**. When the tide is low, you might see **mudflats** and groups of **oysters** (oyster beds) along the mudflat edges. And when the tide is high, this brackish water flows over the land creating **salt marshes**, a good place to look for **egrets** and other marsh birds.

Estuaries are home to more young and growing plants and animals than any other habitat or ecosystem in the world. Many of the fish, **shrimp**, and other ocean animals spend the early part of their lives in estuaries. **Clams** and other **shellfish** live in the mudflats. And migrating birds all over the world spend some time in estuaries as they feed on some of the plants and animals found there.

Prepare yourself for a great adventure as you begin to discover seashore life. But before you go, there are some rules you must follow to protect the life at the seashore and to keep yourself safe:

1. When you're exploring the seashore, try not to step on any live animals.

2. If you pick up a rock to look underneath it, put it back exactly the way you found it.

3. If you pick up a snail, hermit crab, or other animal, do not keep it out of the water for very long, and remember to put it back where you found it.

4. Always wear shoes with rubber or nonslip soles when exploring rocky shores. Algae and shore plants can be slippery and some shells and rocks can cut your bare feet.

5. Never turn your back on the ocean. A big wave can sneak up on you, or the tide may come in faster than you expected and cut off the way back to dry ground.

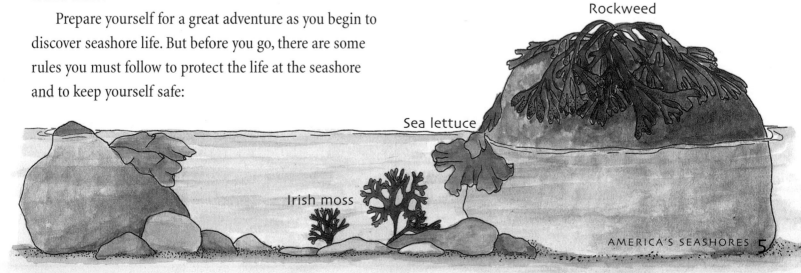

Rockweed

Sea lettuce

Irish moss

Arctic Coast

Arctic Ocean

Arctic Coast

North Pacific Coast

Pacific
Ocean

North Atlantic Coast

South Pacific
Coast

South Atlantic Coast

Atlantic
Ocean

Gulf Coast

Gulf of Mexico

0	500	1,000 miles

km

0	500	1,000

North American Seashores

This book will introduce you to some of the most common or easily found plants and animals of the seashores of North America north of Mexico. Six regions are covered: the North Atlantic Coast, South Atlantic Coast, Gulf Coast, South Pacific Coast, North Pacific Coast, and Arctic Coast.

Some of America's seashores are mostly rocky **coastline**, others have lots of **sandy beaches**, and all the regions have estuaries. But just because regions have the same types of coastline doesn't always mean the same plants and animals can live there. For example, the **red** and **black mangrove trees** that grow in the warm estuaries of the South Atlantic and Gulf Coasts would die in the cold Arctic estuaries that are frozen for many months each year.

Periwinkles, on the other hand, are small snails that live among the plants of rocky shores and estuaries all over North America. By the way, if you pick a periwinkle up out of the water, the snail may shrink back into its shell. Some people say that you can get the snail to come back out by humming to it. Do you know any good songs? Just remember to put the periwinkle back where you found it.

Most of the sandy beaches can be found along the southern Atlantic and Pacific Coasts and along the Gulf Coast. Look at the sand through a magnifying glass, if you can. Some beaches are made up of tiny rocks. Other beaches are made up of ground-up coral and shells.

The best time to visit the seashore depends upon which region you're visiting. Look at the two-page drawings of each region. You should be able to find the plants and animals shown there from at least spring through fall. In warmer areas, such as the South Atlantic, Gulf, and South Pacific Coasts, the same plants and animals might be there all year long.

And for those of you who don't want to get your feet wet by actually visiting the seashore, you can explore these incredible places just by turning the pages of this book. Enjoy your journey.

Red mangrove

North American Seashores

Sitka spruce

Bluff—
Trees may grow along the top of these steep rock or dirt cliffs at the edge of the sea. During breeding season, **puffins** and other seabirds make their nests on rock ledges above or on a cliff's face.

The seashore has many different habitats. Not all animals can be found in each habitat, so knowing something about what makes each area different may help you enjoy your trips to the coast even more. For example, would you like to see some spiny **sea urchins**? Then you need to visit a rocky shore during low tide. How about **fiddler crabs**? Go to salt marshes as the tide goes down and look for the crabs and their holes in sandy or muddy areas.

The drawings on these two pages shows some of the more common seashore habitats.

Splash zone

Barnacles

High-tide zone

Mussels

Mid-tide zone

Sea urchins

Low-tide zone

Seal

Oysters

Eelgrass

Rockweed

Anemone

Mudflat

Rocky shore—
Look for pools in the rocks (tide pools) left behind as the ocean level goes down during low tide. Many plants and animals that cannot live very long out of water, such as Irish moss and **sea stars**, are found in and around these pools. Large rocky beaches and ledges are also exposed during low tide and are used by **seals** and **sea lions** as resting places, or haul outs.

Splash zone—
The splash zone is the area that gets wet only when ocean waves splash or spray the shore. Barnacles live here.

High-tide zone—
The high-tide zone is the area covered by water only during the highest tides. **Limpets** are found here.

Mid-tide zone—
On most beaches this part of the shore, the mid-tide zone, is usually covered and uncovered by water at least twice a day. Rockweed and mussels are found here.

Low-tide zone—
The low-tide zone is the area closest to the ocean waves and can be seen only when the water is at its lowest level each day. Look for sea urchins and sea anemones.

Sky—

Don't forget to look up at the sky, even though it's not an actual habitat. You may see puffins and **murres** in the sky around cliffs and bluffs, especially in the spring and summer when they are raising babies. In the sky above sandy and rocky beaches, look for terns and gulls. And just beyond the beach and waves, you may see **brown pelicans** flying by.

Gull

Sea oats

Egret

Beach pea

Brown pelican

Pickleweed or Glasswort

Dune—

Dunes are formed by sand that the wind blows up into large piles or hills. Dunes are found above the high-tide line along some sandy beaches. **Sea oats** and **beach grass** help keep the sand on the dunes from blowing away. **Ghost crabs** may have their burrows here.

Salt marsh

Clam

Estuary—

An estuary is where the freshwater from a river flows into the salt water of the sea. Here the salty water rises and falls with the tides, covering and uncovering the fine silt of the mudflats and washing over the plants of the higher salt marshes along the edge. Salt marshes also occur along quiet shores behind barrier islands and at the edge of some bays and inlets. **Salt grass** and **pickleweed** grow in salt marshes. Mudflats may be home to clams, burrowing shrimp, and crabs. Mudflats also attract egrets, who use their long bills to hunt for food in the mud.

Sandy beach—

Beach wrack is the line of dried seaweeds, bits of driftwood, small shells, etc., left behind by the waves at the edge of the high-tide line. Look in and under the beach wrack for **beetles, flies**, and other small animals. **Mole crabs** and **coquina clams** live under the sand where the waves keep the beach wet. Birds such as **plovers** and **terns** may nest along sandy beaches.

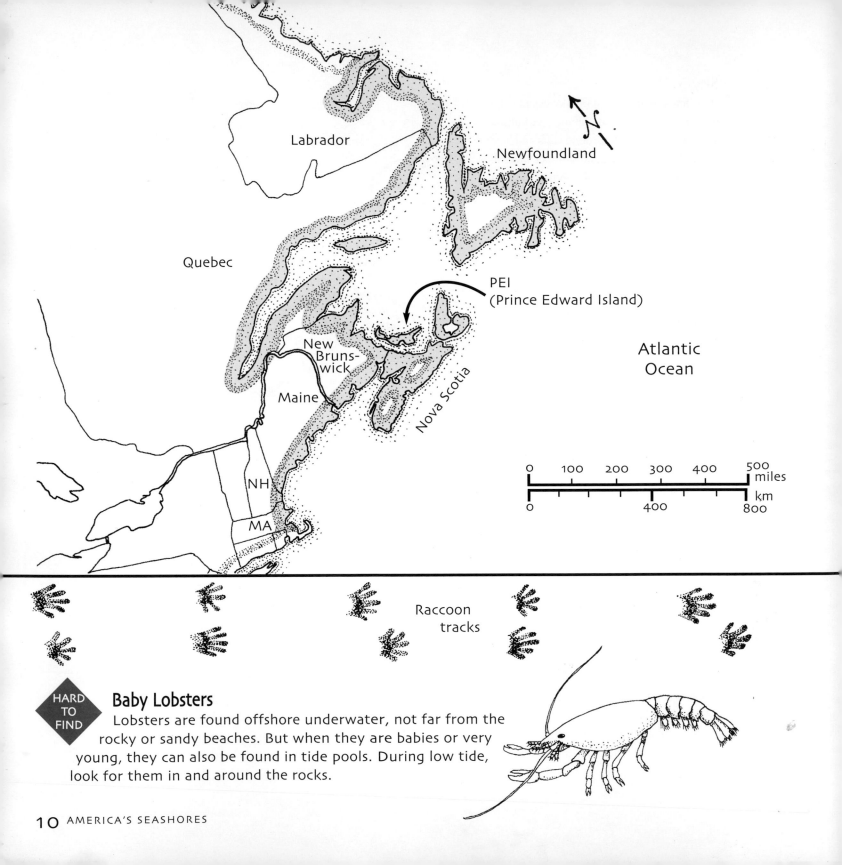

Labrador

Newfoundland

N

Quebec

PEI
(Prince Edward Island)

New
Bruns-
wick

Atlantic
Ocean

Maine

Nova Scotia

NH

MA

| 0 | 100 | 200 | 300 | 400 | 500 miles |

| 0 | | 400 | | 800 km |

Raccoon
tracks

HARD
TO
FIND

Baby Lobsters

Lobsters are found offshore underwater, not far from the rocky or sandy beaches. But when they are babies or very young, they can also be found in tide pools. During low tide, look for them in and around the rocks.

North Atlantic Coast

The North Atlantic Coast is a region of rocky shores, strong ocean storms, and crashing waves. Forests of trees grow out to the very edge of cliffs alongside the sea and **seabirds** nest on rocky ledges 100 feet or more above the ocean waves.

You will see two common colors of the splash zone here on the rocky coast: black and bright yellow. The black is a type of blue-green algae that is crusty when dry but very slippery when wet (be careful!). The yellow is the **sunburst lichen** and grows as blotches on the rocks. Lichens are combinations of algae and **fungi** (mushrooms are a type of fungi) that come in many colors, including yellow, orange, and gray-green. You can find them on rocks and trees in many different habitats, not just on the seashore.

At mid- to low tide, you may see huge areas of the rocky shoreline covered in olive green or brownish colored algae, called rockweed, and the light, purplish red Irish moss. Animals such as the **rock crab** and the **green crab** (the most common crab in the region) live among these seaweeds, hidden from view.

Beaches, barrier islands, estuaries, protected bays, and salt marshes can also be found here. While you're walking along a sandy beach check for **mermaid's purses** that have

Moon snail

washed up on shore. These are actually the empty egg cases of **sharks**, **stingrays**, or **skates**, a type of stingray.

Along the beach you may also see some brownish, flat, comma-shaped objects that look a lot like pieces of hard root-beer candy. They come from **moon snails** and were used to plug the opening to the snail, protecting the animal inside from predators or the drying air. And if you spot what looks like a crooked, pale, orangish red hand with fingers pointing upward, you'll know how this sponge, called **dead man's fingers**, got its name.

Take a walk along the calmer brackish water of this region's estuaries. You will find a few bushes that have been especially useful to people and animals. A shrub called **shadbush** got its name because a fish called the **American shad** can be found in the nearby rivers when the shrub is in flower. **Bayberry** has a waxy covering around its fruit that used to be used for making candles. Now only the scent, or smell, of bayberry is used in candle making. And **winterberry** is an important source of food for wildlife.

So stand on a rocky shore and feel the salt spray on your face. Then take the time to explore the bays, beaches, and tide pools of this rugged coast.

Shadbush

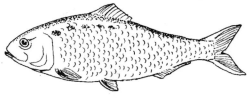

American shad

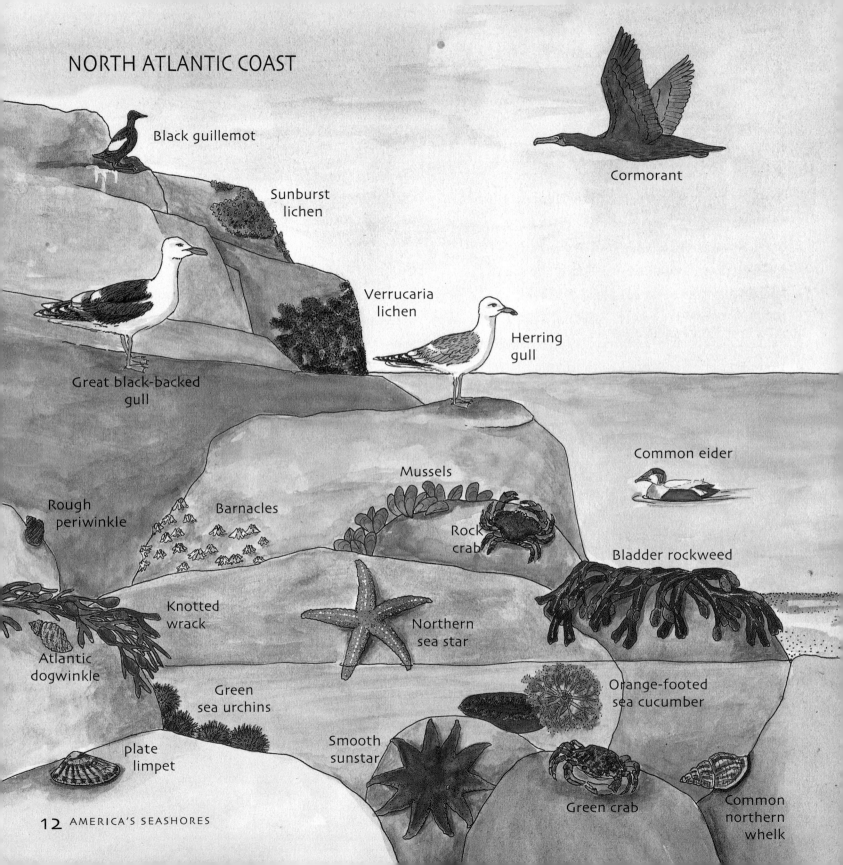

NORTH ATLANTIC COAST

Black guillemot

Cormorant

Sunburst lichen

Verrucaria lichen

Herring gull

Great black-backed gull

Common eider

Mussels

Rough periwinkle

Barnacles

Rock crab

Bladder rockweed

Knotted wrack

Northern sea star

Atlantic dogwinkle

Green sea urchins

Orange-footed sea cucumber

plate limpet

Smooth sunstar

Green crab

Common northern whelk

Osprey

Common tern

Humpback whale

Beach grass

Raccoon

Winterberry

Harbor seal

Harbor porpoise

Beach pea

Salt hay

Bayberry

Horseshoe crab

Moon snail

Hermit crab in Common periwinkle shell

Irish moss

Eelgrass

Yellowlegs

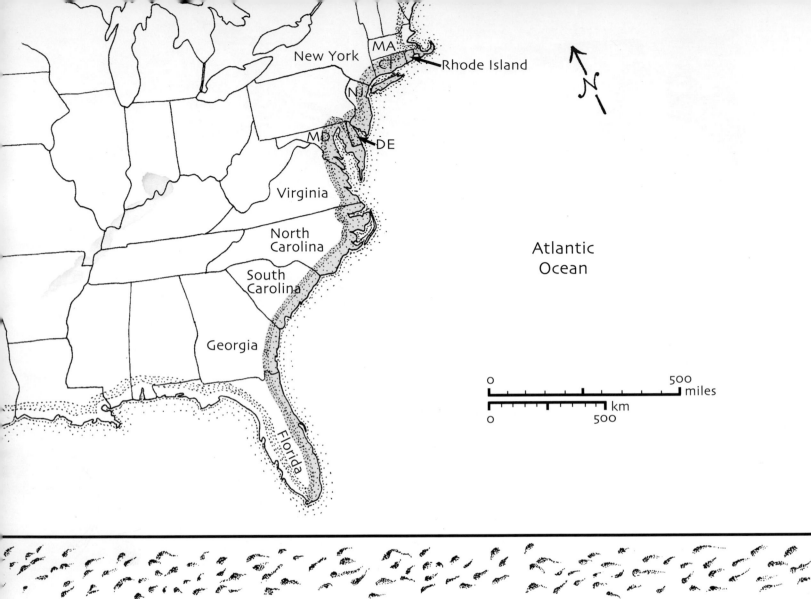

New York

MA

CT

→ Rhode Island

NJ

MD

DE

Virginia

North
Carolina

South
Carolina

Georgia

Florida

N

Atlantic
Ocean

| 0 | | | | | 500 |
miles
| 0 | | | 500 | | |
km

Ghost crab tracks

HARD
TO
FIND

Ghost Crabs

These 2-inch-wide (5.1 cm) crabs are common on sandy beaches above
the high-tide line. But because they are mostly nocturnal, coming out at
night to hunt for food, you may only see their burrow holes and
tracks during the day. Watch for ghost crabs on clear nights with
bright moonlight, when their pale yellow or grayish color
blends in with the dry sand, making them appear ghostlike.

South Atlantic Coast

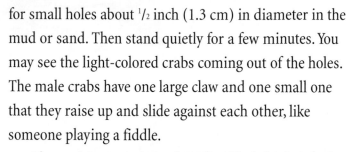

Coquina clams

Actual size

One of the best places to enjoy the seashore in this region is from the top of a **primary dune** among the sea oats and beach grass. This is the sand dune at the edge of the ocean beach, just above the flat, sandy beaches that are common here. Look for **beach pea**, with its purplish pink flowers growing on the dune slope that faces the ocean.

During low tide, walk along the beach and you might see little flat shells with bands of bright colors lying on the sand at the edge of each incoming ocean wave. These are coquina clams. They live just beneath the sand and eat tiny bits of food brought in with the water. As soon as each wave goes away, the clams burrow into the sand again.

High tide can also be an interesting time to visit the shore. **Horseshoe crabs**, which have lived on the Earth for millions of years, come onto some of the sandy beaches in the spring, during the highest tides, to lay eggs. When the eggs hatch, the young horseshoe crabs wait until the next highest tide to swim or float back into the sea. (By the way, horseshoe crabs are not real crabs. They are more closely related to spiders.)

Barrier islands are a common feature of the southern Atlantic coastline. And the salt marshes on the mainland-facing side of some of these islands are good places to find fiddler crabs. During low tide, check

for small holes about $^1/_2$ inch (1.3 cm) in diameter in the mud or sand. Then stand quietly for a few minutes. You may see the light-colored crabs coming out of the holes. The male crabs have one large claw and one small one that they raise up and slide against each other, like someone playing a fiddle.

If you visit an estuary when the tide is high, it looks like a river or lake with plants growing right out of the water. But during low tide, you'll see that the plants are on the tops of muddy banks. Look for oysters growing along the bank's sides and for birds such as **yellowlegs** poking their narrow bills into the mud and eating the small animals that live there. The largest estuary in the United States is 200-mile-long Chesapeake Bay, along the states of Maryland and Virginia.

Have you ever heard of a "walking tree"? That's what some people call the red mangrove, which grows along the warm coastline of southern Florida. With long, curved roots hanging down into the shallow water, it looks a bit like it's walking. The roots help support the tree and also provide underwater hiding places for small fish, crabs, snails, and other marine life. Farther onshore is the black mangrove, whose root tips stick up through the mud. These fingerlike roots help the plant breathe in the water-soaked ground.

You will never run out of interesting places to explore or amazing plants and animals to discover along this seashore.

Fiddler crab
Actual size

SOUTH ATLANTIC COAST

Brown pelican

Great black-backed gull

Sea oats

Dusty miller

Beach grass

Sea rocket

Herring gull

Channeled whelk

Beach pea

Knobbed whelk

Moon snail

Quahog

Hermit crab

Sanderling

Great blue heron

Osprey

Salt marsh bulrush

Cordgrass

Great egret

Needlerush

Raccoon

Glasswort or Pickleweed

Black skimmer

Snowy egret

Sea oxeye daisy

Willet

American oystercatcher

Yellowlegs

Oysters

Sea purslane

Dowitcher

Mussels

Horseshoe crab

Blue crab

Sea lettuce on Clam shell

Laughing gull

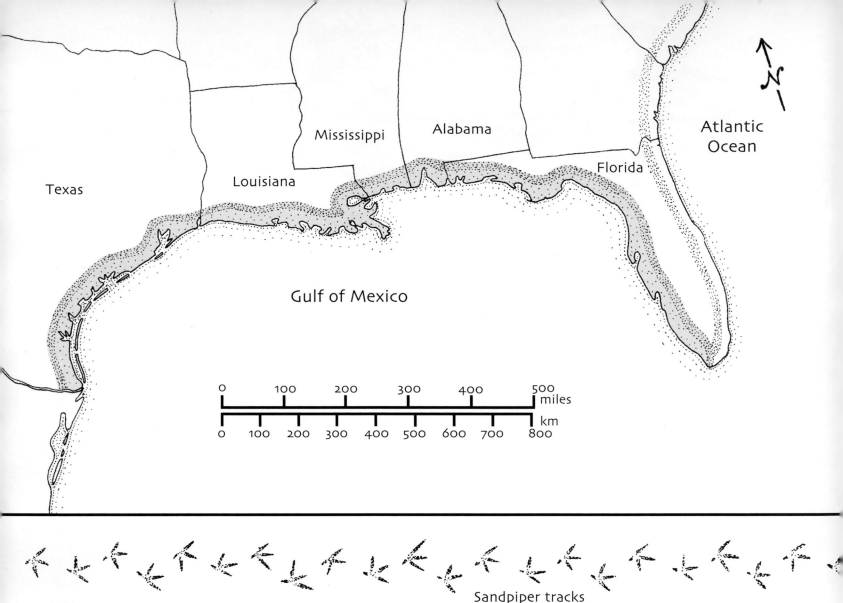

Texas
Louisiana
Mississippi
Alabama
Florida
Atlantic Ocean
Gulf of Mexico

N

| 0 | 100 | 200 | 300 | 400 | 500 |
miles

km
| 0 | 100 | 200 | 300 | 400 | 500 | 600 | 700 | 800 |

Sandpiper tracks

HARD TO FIND

Sea Turtles

Five of the seven types of sea turtles in the world live in the Gulf of Mexico. These five are the loggerhead, leatherback, hawksbill, green, and Kemp's ridley. All of these sea turtles are threatened or endangered species and are protected by law.

Although sea turtles live in the ocean, they are born on land. When a female sea turtle is ready to lay her eggs, she crawls onto the same sandy beach where she was born. She picks a spot above the high-tide line and digs a pit with her back legs. Then she lays her eggs in the hole, covers them with sand, and returns to the sea.

Gulf Coast

Seaside sparrow on cordgrass

The Gulf Coast is a calm, warm coastline. Long, flat beaches, barrier islands, and estuaries are common here. Most of the time the beach waves are small, and even the difference between high tide and low tide is small, usually only 2 feet (0.6 m).

Sometimes storms create larger waves and churn up the sandy bottom. That's when you should go **beachcombing**. During low tide after a storm check for empty shells, seaweeds, and other material the waves may have left on the beach. You might find a **channeled whelk**, the official state shell of Texas. You might also see bluish or clear jellylike objects on the sand among the shells. Do not touch these. They may be dead **Portuguese man-of-wars**, or jellyfish such as **moon jellies** or **sea nettles**. The parts on their body that were used to sting the fish they caught for food may still sting or hurt you, even though the animal is dead.

Portuguese man-of-war

Also along the beaches of the Gulf Coast are terns. These birds are common on sandy shores and sometimes make their nests right out in the open on the sand. When you first see them, you may think they are gulls. But terns have more slender bodies, pointy bills, and forked tails that are visible when they're flying.

The longest barrier island in the world is found here: Padre Island, Texas, which is 113 miles (182 km) long. This is also where you will find Padre Island National Seashore, whose 100-mile-long beach is the longest natural (undeveloped) ocean beach in the United States.

One of the world's greatest estuaries, the Mississippi Delta, is found where the Mississippi River empties into the Gulf of Mexico. Silt and mud brought by the river pile up along the shore and help create one of the largest salt marshes in the United States. Listen for the buzzing song of the **seaside sparrow**, whose nest is in the **cordgrass**, one of the most common plants of these salt marshes. If you look closely at the cordgrass just above the water's surface, you may see periwinkle snails on its stems.

If you have a chance to take a boat ride along the eastern part of the Gulf Coast, look into the water and along the shores for **alligators**. Although they prefer the freshwater of wetlands farther inland, you may see alligators in salt marshes, where a plant called **needlerush** is found.

Now all that's left is for you to peer into these salt marshes and estuaries for the birds and other animals that live there. Or you can take off your shoes and stroll along the sandy beaches looking for shells. The seashores of this region are waiting for you.

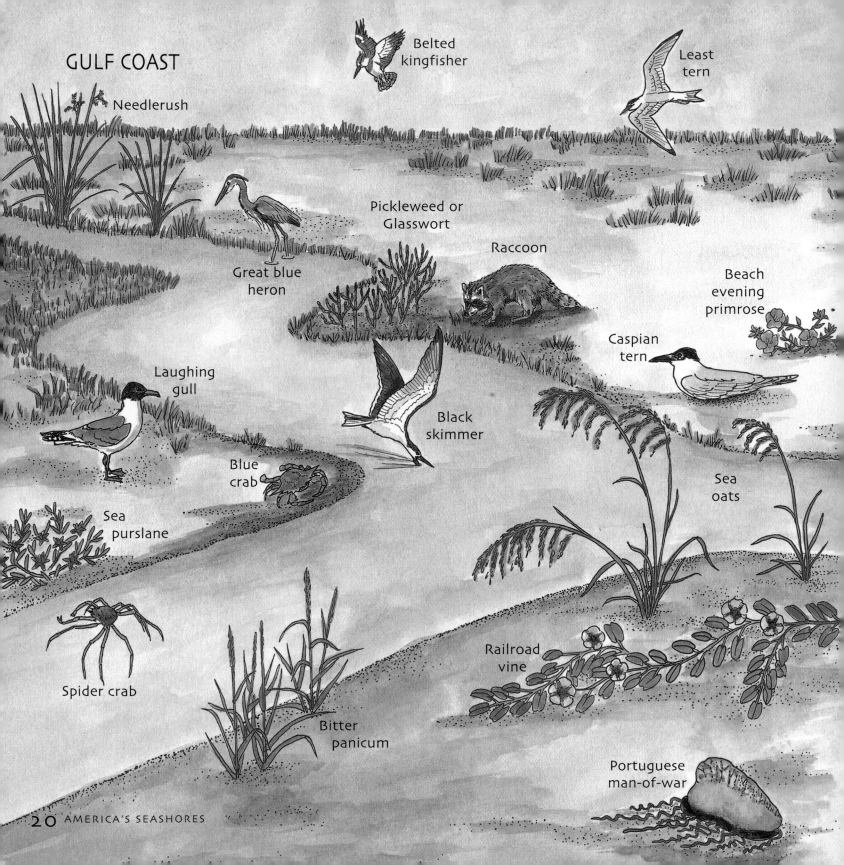

GULF COAST

Belted kingfisher

Least tern

Needlerush

Pickleweed or Glasswort

Raccoon

Beach evening primrose

Great blue heron

Caspian tern

Laughing gull

Black skimmer

Sea oats

Blue crab

Sea purslane

Spider crab

Railroad vine

Bitter panicum

Portuguese man-of-war

Herring gull

Osprey

White ibis

Black mangrove

Brown pelican

Cormorant

Red mangrove

Great egret

Sanderling

Snowy plover

Snowy egret

Lightning whelk

Sargassum weed

Cannonball jellyfish

Royal tern

By-the-wind sailor

Hermit crab

Stingray

Mermaid's purse

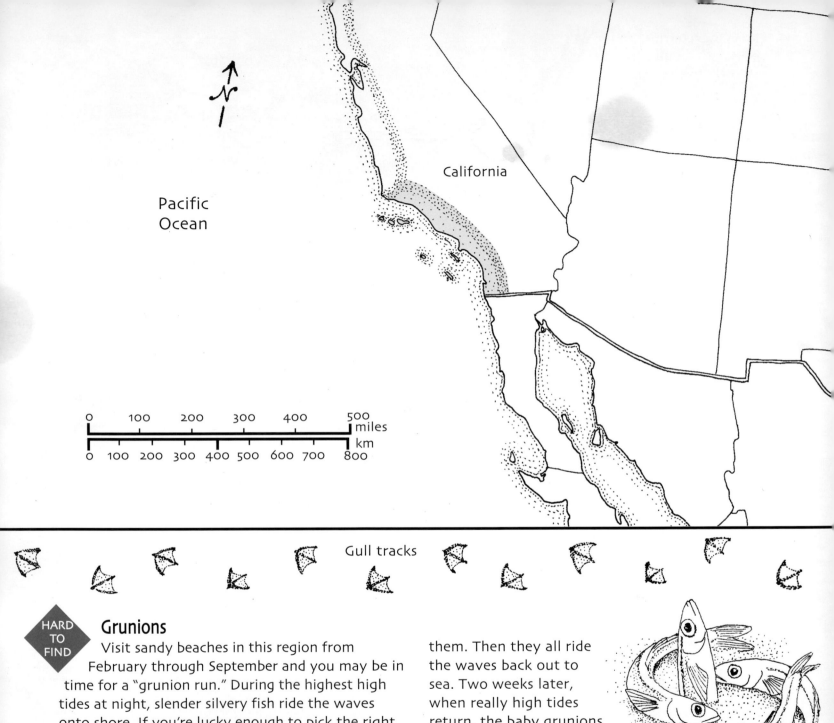

Pacific
Ocean

California

Gull tracks

Grunions

HARD TO FIND

Visit sandy beaches in this region from February through September and you may be in time for a "grunion run." During the highest high tides at night, slender silvery fish ride the waves onto shore. If you're lucky enough to pick the right night and the right beach, you'll see hundreds of these grunions. The females dig into the wet sand and lay their eggs while the males curve around them. Then they all ride the waves back out to sea. Two weeks later, when really high tides return, the baby grunions have hatched and are ready to ride their own waves back out to sea.

South Pacific Coast

Much of the seashore area in the South Pacific coastal region is no longer natural. Houses line the sandy beaches and boat harbors sit where there were once estuaries. More than 13 million people live within a one-hour drive of the South Pacific Coast. But along rocky shores and protected beaches, you can still find wonderful examples of the plants and animals that live here.

Visit rocky tide pools during low tide. The volcano-shaped **keyhole limpets** and hairy-edged **chitons** are usually on the tops and sides of large rocks. Bright orange or purple ochre sea stars keep out of the sun by clinging to the wet undersides of rocks, and crabs stay hidden in narrow cracks. Sometimes there are so many purple sea urchins in a tide pool that the entire bottom of the pool looks purple.

Pieces of **giant kelp** and other seaweeds are often washed up in piles on beaches by the waves. If you look closely, you may notice what look like small insects flying and jumping around on the pile. Those are probably **kelp flies** and **beach fleas**. Lift up a pile and check for beetles and other insects eating bits of food or enjoying the cool shade.

White and **gray California gulls** are common at the beaches. And as waves crash over the sand, shorebirds such as **dowitchers** and **sanderlings** run back and forth hunting for food.

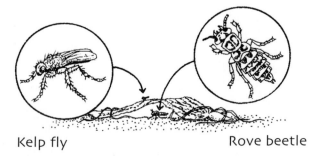

Kelp fly   Rove beetle

Even though this region doesn't get much rain, there are still estuaries where rivers flow to the sea. One of the largest is the Tijuana Estuary, which lies along the border of Mexico and the United States. Pickleweed and **saltwort** are found in the salt marshes, and birds such as **great blue herons** and **willets** hunt for food in the tide pools and mudflats.

Also in the mudflats, the **innkeeper worm** makes a U-shaped burrow. This worm is very common, but its whole life is spent underground, which makes it hard to

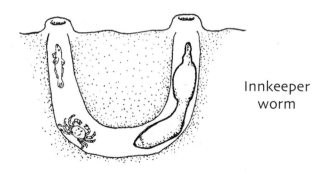

Innkeeper worm

find. How did it get its name? Inside the innkeeper worm's burrow live many different animals, including the **pea crab** and the **arrow goby**, making it sort of like an underground hotel or inn.

Sometimes you have to look a bit harder to discover the wonders of the seashore. There are many places waiting to be explored.

SOUTH PACIFIC COAST

Brown pelican

Dune grass

Beach grass

Giant kelp bed

Great blue heron

Beach morning glory

Cordgrass

Western gull

Great egret

Black turban snails

Wavy turban shell

Owl limpet

Eelgrass

Marsh rosemary

Rough limpet

Pickleweed or Glasswort

Keyhole limpet

Lined shore crab

Cormorants

Caspian tern

Harbor seal

Rockweed

Surf grass

Snowy egret

Giant kelp

Silverweed

Feather boa kelp

Barnacles

Brown sea hare

Mussels

Crustose coralline algae

Purple sea urchin

Goose barnacles

Purple shore crab

Hermit crab in Turban snail shell

Aggregating anemone

Giant green anemone

Mossy chiton

Red sea urchin

Sculpin

Turkish towel

Sea lettuce

Ochre sea star

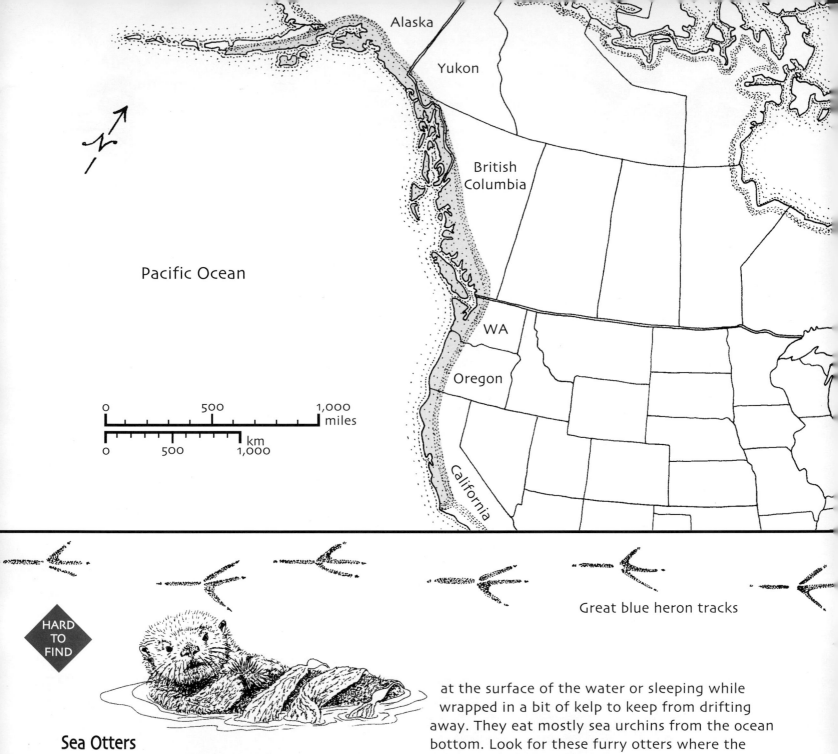

Alaska

Yukon

British Columbia

Pacific Ocean

WA

Oregon

California

| 0 | 500 | 1,000 |
miles

| 0 | 500 | 1,000 |
km

Great blue heron tracks

HARD TO FIND

Sea Otters

Sea otters may live their entire lives in the ocean but close to shore. You might see them swimming at the surface of the water or sleeping while wrapped in a bit of kelp to keep from drifting away. They eat mostly sea urchins from the ocean bottom. Look for these furry otters where the tops of kelp forest plants float on the surface of the water.

North Pacific Coast

Waves crash against cliffs, sending ocean spray into the **Sitka spruce** perched on the cliff tops. **Bald eagles** may be sitting in these trees, waiting to fly down and catch a live fish from the ocean or pick at a dead one washed up on shore.

As the ocean waves slowly break down the coastline, rocky or sandy beaches develop points of land sticking out into the ocean called **headlands**. Sometimes these headlands become tree-covered islands as the sea eats away the land between the headland and the **mainland** shore.

Many of these islands are full of marine life. Murres and other seabirds nest there because they are protected from coyotes, raccoons, and other animals that might prey on their eggs and baby birds. The rocky shores above the high-tide line on the islands are often used by harbor seals and sea lions as haul outs, which are areas where seals rest when they're out of the water.

Along the mainland, many beaches and bays, or **inlets**, are rocky. During low tide, look in tide pools left behind for a small fish called a blenny. You may see them swimming around giant green anemones or the many-armed sunflower sea star.

Also during low tide, on the rocks where the waves are crashing, you can see plants that look like small palm trees bending back and forth in the surf. These are **sea palms**, a type of brown algae or kelp. Sometimes sea palms break loose from the rocks and are brought to shore by the waves. When this happens, you can get a good look at this interesting kelp. Otherwise, just look for it from the safety of the beach. The crashing waves can be very dangerous if you try to see sea palms where they grow naturally.

Pickleweed, salt grass, and **arrowgrass** are all common salt marsh plants of the estuaries in the North Pacific coastal region. When the tide is out and mudflats in the estuaries are exposed you might see small holes with what look like little pieces of brown gravel nearby. Those are the burrow openings of **ghost shrimp** and their "poop."

Along the coast of Oregon is a huge area of sand dunes about 54 miles (87 km) long. This is the largest area of coastal sand dunes on the Earth. **Dune grass**, **beach grass**, and **beach morning glory** all grow on the dunes closest to the sea.

This is one of the longest coastal regions in North America, with enough variety to keep you interested no matter how many times you return to explore.

Sitka spruce

Ghost shrimp

NORTH PACIFIC COAST

Shore pine

Osprey

Dune grass

Gray whale with calf

Seashore lupine

Beach grass

Harbor seal

Steller sea lion

Beach evening primrose

Bull kelp

Great blue heron

Western gull

Thatched barnacles

Mussels

Beach morning glory

Beach pea

Salt marsh dodder on Pickleweed

Limpets

Goose barnacles

Sponge

Purple sea urchin

Hermit crab

Red ribbon worm

Sculpin

Gumboot chiton

Red sea urchin

Bald eagle

Black turnstone

Cormorant

Sitka spruce

California sea lion

Ochre sea star

Gumweed

Sea palm

Surf grass

Rockweed

Black oystercatcher

Black katy chiton

Purple shore crab

Seaside daisy

Barnacles

Blood star

Lined shore crab

Agreggating anemone

By-the-wind sailor

Black turban snail

Green sea urchins

Turkish towel

Sunflower star

Giant green anemone

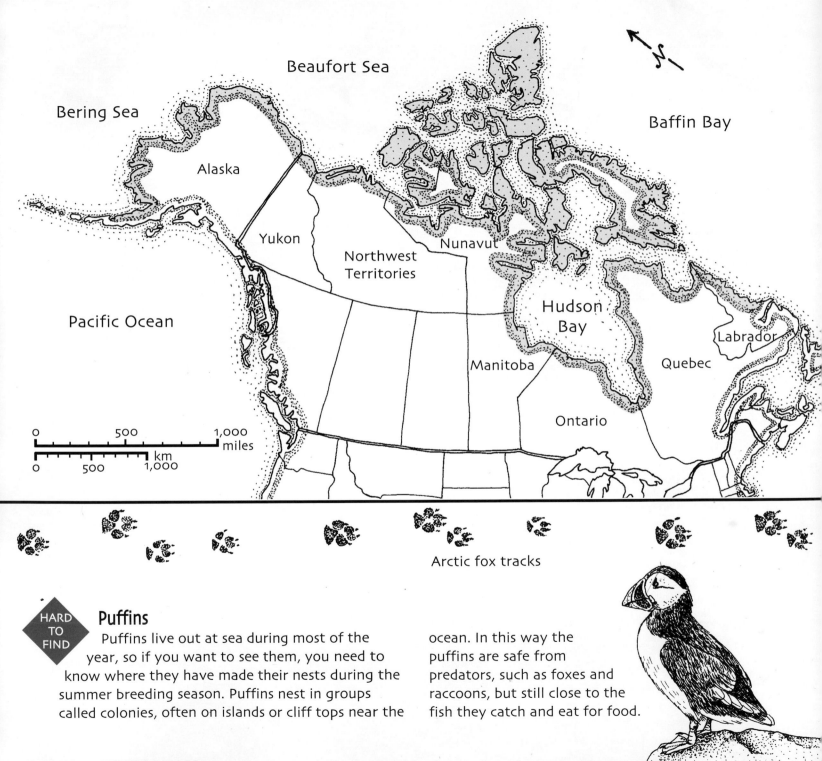

Beaufort Sea

Bering Sea

Alaska

Baffin Bay

Yukon

Nunavut

Northwest
Territories

Pacific Ocean

Hudson
Bay

Manitoba

Labrador

Quebec

Ontario

| 0 | 500 | 1,000 miles |
| 0 | 500 | 1,000 km |

Arctic fox tracks

Puffins

HARD TO FIND

Puffins live out at sea during most of the year, so if you want to see them, you need to know where they have made their nests during the summer breeding season. Puffins nest in groups called colonies, often on islands or cliff tops near the ocean. In this way the puffins are safe from predators, such as foxes and raccoons, but still close to the fish they catch and eat for food.

Arctic Coast

Arctic char

Imagine a coastline that is all white. The winter snow on the beach meets the ice and snow over the shallow water off the coast, making the shore and sea appear as one. Then, for a few months each year during late spring and summer, the days become warmer, the snow melts, and this white world is transformed.

Plants begin to grow through the melting snow. Mosquitoes fill the air above salt marshes and other brackish water. **Eelgrass** begins to grow and cover the bottom of muddy bays and marshes. And all across the Arctic, migrating birds arrive to breed, nest, and raise their young.

If there was a prize for the most amazing story of a migrating bird, the **arctic tern** would win. These birds start their trip to the Arctic nesting grounds from Antarctica, near the South Pole, 12,000 miles (19,320 km) away. And at the end of the summer, when they have finished raising their young, the terns fly back to Antarctica. From the South Pole to the North Pole and back again, no other bird migrates farther in one year than the arctic tern.

Much of the Arctic Coast is made up of steep-sloped rocky shores or gravel and sand beaches, where few plants grow. Birds such as **kittiwakes** and murres make nests on rocky cliffs, while common terns and arctic terns lay their eggs right on the sandy beach.

An animal you might not think of as living at the edge of the ocean, the **arctic fox**, may be seen hunting along the beach in summer, eating small crabs at the water's edge or stealing the eggs of nesting birds. Not far from where the fox hunts, a fish called an **arctic char** may be swimming in the shallow water. And a bit farther out to sea, but still visible from shore, look for **ringed seals** or white **beluga whales**.

Midsummer is a noisy time in bays and salt marshes, where ducks and geese raise their young and feast on mussels, eelgrass, crabs, and snails. Arctic marshes do not have the variety of plants and animals that salt marshes farther south do, partly because the chunks of ice that form in the winter scrape along the muddy or sandy bottom and destroy much of what might have been trying to live there.

By summer's end, the eelgrass begins to turn brown and the migrating birds get ready to leave. The Arctic coastline will soon be white again.

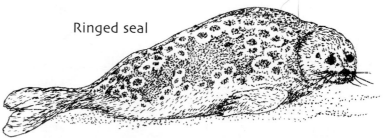

Ringed seal

ARCTIC COAST

Kittiwake

Jaeger

Bowhead whale

Glaucous gull

Murre

Common eider

Black guillemot

Mottled sea star

Plate limpet

Mussels

Hermit crab in Moon snail shell

Frilled anemone

Sunstar

Green sea urchins

Orange-tipped nudibranch

Arctic tern

Polar bear

Beluga whale

Spotted seal

Seashore chamomile

Sea-beach sandwort

Seaside bluebell

Alpine foxtail

Phalarope

Arctic fox

Brant

Arctic daisy

Red-throated loon

Seaside arrowgrass

Blackish oxytrope

Clam

Eelgrass

Common Plants and Animals

Some seashore plants and animals are very common and occur in more than one region. For example, you can find eelgrass, sea stars, and crabs in almost all coastal areas. And gulls or terns will also be found along most rocky or sandy shores.

Information next to the drawings will help you learn where to look and what to look for. Remember that you may need to wait until low tide to see some of the species found in mudflats or tide pools.

Look closely and carefully at everything you find. You might even want to take a small magnifying glass with you when you explore; so much of the seashore world is tiny and easy to miss.

BLACK TURBAN SNAIL

Color: Black; sometimes with white towards the tip.
Size: About 1 inch (2.5 cm) tall and wide.
Food: Algae on rocks.
Notes: Along the Pacific Coast, empty turban shells are a common home for hermit crabs. Look for them in rocky tide pools.

Laughing gull

Herring gull

Goose barnacle

GULLS

Color: Mostly white body with gray wings. Legs and feet are pinkish, yellow, black, orange, or red. Some have black heads. Young gulls are usually mottled brown and white.
Size: Smaller species, such as the laughing gull, are about 13$\frac{1}{2}$–16$\frac{1}{2}$ inches (34–42 cm) long. Larger species, such as the herring gull, can be 21–30 inches (53–76 cm) long.
Food: Almost anything from fish to bird eggs to potato chips and other human food left near trash cans.
Notes: Some gulls will carry a mussel, or other shellfish, into the air and drop it onto a rock or the ground so that the shell breaks and the gull can eat the animal inside.

BARNACLES

Color: White to grayish tan.
Size: From tiny species $\frac{1}{4}$ inch (6mm) across and $\frac{1}{8}$ inch (4mm) high, to larger species 1$\frac{1}{2}$ inches (3.8 cm) across and 2$\frac{1}{2}$ inches (6.4 cm) high. The common goose barnacle is about 2$\frac{3}{4}$ inches (7.0 cm) across at the tip, but can be up to 6 inches (15.2 cm) long because of its long neck or stalk.
Food: Small bits of plants and animals drifting by in the water.
Notes: Northern rock barnacles, goose or leaf barnacles, and acorn barnacles are only a few of the many kinds found in the intertidal zone. Look at barnacles when they're underwater in tide pools and you may see the wavy feelers that catch the food particles the barnacles eat.

HARBOR SEAL

Color: Gray or brownish with dark spots.
Size: 4–5½ feet (1.2–1.7 m) long.
Food: Fish.
Notes: During low tide, you may see these seals hauled out, or resting, on rocks above the reach of the waves. Other times you may just see the harbor seals' heads showing above the water as the seals rest vertically in the ocean near shore.

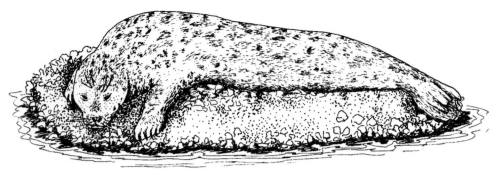

MUSSELS

Color: Very dark purplish gray to black or dark blue.
Size: The California mussel of the Pacific Coast can grow up to 10 inches (25.4 cm) long. The blue mussel of the Atlantic Coast may grow up to 4 inches (10.2 cm) long.
Food: Small bits of plants and animals drifting by in the water.
Notes: Look for mussels in the mid- to low-tide zones of rocky shores and estuaries or bays. Light brown–colored hairs, called byssal threads, hold the mussels to rocks.

PERIWINKLE SNAIL

Color: Tan to brown or black; some have dark brown stripes and markings. Algae growing on shells may give them a greenish color.
Size: ½ to 1½ inch (1.3–3.8 cm) long.
Food: Algae found on rocks.
Notes: There are many different kinds of perwinkles. Marsh periwinkles are found on plants in salt marshes—look on the leaves or stems above or at the water's surface. Rough perwinkles and common perwinkles (introduced from Europe; not native plants) are found along the coast in some rocky intertidal zones.

Marsh periwinkle

Checkered periwinkle

CLAMS

Color: Light tan or white; sometimes brownish. Many have darker brown markings such as spots or stripes. The small coquina clams may have pink or brown bands and purplish or yellow shells.
Size: Commonly 1–2 inches (2.5–5.1 cm) wide. The large quahogs of the Atlantic, Gulf, and Pacific Coasts are 4–5 inches (10.2–12.7 cm) wide or more.
Food: Tiny pieces of floating plants or other organic, or natural, material.

Notes: Clam shells are bivalves, two shells that are hinged together. They are usually smooth or with ridges. You may not see a live clam unless you dig for them in sand or mud. But clam shells—often only one side—are found washed up on beaches or left behind after gulls or other animals have eaten the animal that lived inside.

Giant Atlantic cockle

Coquina clam

Quahog

Crabs and Other Arthropods

ROCK CRAB

Color: Brownish on the Atlantic Coast and purplish on the Pacific Coast.

Size: $2^1/_2$–$3^1/_2$ inches (6.4–8.9 cm) long and 3–5 inches (7.6–12.7 cm) wide.

Food: Marine animals and sea lettuce.

Notes: Look for these crabs on sandy or rocky shores. They are common among kelp and seaweeds and in tide pools from the high-tide zone to the low-tide zone.

MOLE CRAB

Color: Pale gray or tan.

Size: 1–$1^1/_2$ inches (2.5–3.8 cm) long.

Food: Tiny marine life floating in the seawater.

Notes: Look for tiny holes in the swash zone. If you dig quickly into the sand with your hands, you may find some mole crabs. They won't hurt you and will probably scurry off your hands and back into the wet sand as quickly as possible. Mole crabs are sometimes called sand crabs.

BEACH FLEA

Color: Gray to reddish brown or white.

Size: Up to about 1 inch (2.5 cm) long.

Food: Seaweeds.

Notes: Also called sand hoppers, beach fleas are not actually fleas and do not bite people. But they can jump very far and can be found on sandy beaches under or near piles of washed-up seaweeds.

HERMIT CRABS

Color: If you can see the crab's legs, they may be whitish, tan, brown, reddish, orangish, a shade of green, or almost black, depending upon the type of hermit crab. Look really closely and you may see lines or spots of other colors including blue, deep orange, or white.

Size: Hermit crabs found in tide pools usually live in small shells up to about $^3/_4$–1 inch (1.9–2.5 cm) wide or tall. The body of the giant hermit crab can be up to $4^3/_4$ inches (12.1 cm) long, so it's shell home has to be big too. It lives along areas of the South Atlantic and Gulf Coasts with sandy bottoms.

Food: Tiny plants and animals (even dead animals).

Notes: A shell moving fairly quickly across the bottom of a tide pool is probably a hermit crab. You may see legs sticking out of the shell. Hermit crabs have soft bodies, so they use empty shells from other animals that fit and protect their body until they grow too big and need to find a larger shell.

MOSQUITOES

Color: Brownish; many have dark and light bands on legs.

Size: About $^1/_4$ inch (0.6 cm) long.

Food: Adult females feed on blood. Adult males drink flower nectar.

Notes: Salt marsh mosquitoes may be common along the edge of bays and estuaries, especially if plants are growing in the

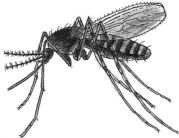

water along the shore. Some mosquito species can spread disease. They are especially common during the warm weather of late spring and summer.

Seashells, Sea Stars, and Sea Urchins

Owl limpet

SEA URCHINS

Color: Purple, greenish, or red.

Size: From 2–5 inches (5.1–12.7 cm) across, depending upon species.

Food: Mostly algae such as sea lettuce and kelp, but will also eat dead fish.

Notes: Sea urchins are found in the tide pools of many rocky shores. Look for them in the mid- to low-tide zone. The purple sea urchins of the Pacific Coast may be found in holes in the rock that the urchins have eaten away themselves.

CHITONS

Color: Brownish, tan, black, or green, depending upon species.

Size: Most are 1–4 inches (2.5–10.2 cm) long. The Giant Pacific chiton, or "gumboot" chiton, of the Pacific Coast is the largest chiton in the world and can grow up to 13 inches (33.0 cm) long.

Food: Mostly algae growing on rocks.

Notes: Found sucked onto rocks in intertidal zones, usually in shady areas out of direct sunlight. Look closely, you may be able to see the eight plates on the chiton's back surrounded by a rubbery edge called a girdle.

LIMPETS

Color: Usually brownish; some have darker brown or light-colored bands or spots.

Size: Most grow to about 1 inch (2.5 cm) long. The giant keyhole limpet of the South Pacific Coast can be 5–6 inches (12.7–15.2) long.

Food: Algae growing on rocks.

Notes: Limpets are one of the most common animals of the rocky intertidal zone. Some limpets are called "keyhole" limpets because they have a hole at the very top of their shell. This actually makes them look a bit like a tiny volcano. If you touch a limpet, it will probably suck hard onto the rock where you found it. Do not try to pry limpets off rocks; you may hurt them or break their shells.

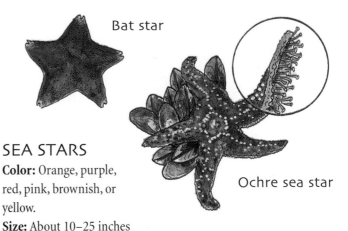

Bat star

Ochre sea star

SEA STARS

Color: Orange, purple, red, pink, brownish, or yellow.

Size: About 10–25 inches (25.4–63.5 cm) across.

Food: Mostly shellfish such as mussels and clams. May eat sea urchins.

Notes: These animals are also called starfish, but they are not fish. Hundreds of tube feet on the sea star's underside help it move along the surface and grip the sides of shellfish, which it pulls open to eat.

Birds

BROWN PELICAN

Color: Grayish brown body with white to yellowish head. Brownish bill may have some orange.

Size: A very large bird. About 4¼ feet (1.3 m) long with a wingspan that measures more than 6 feet (1.8 m) from tip to tip.

Food: Fish.

Notes: Brown pelicans catch their food by diving from the air into the water and scooping up fish and seawater. They have pouches under their bills that can stretch to hold as much volume as five 2-liter soda bottles.

TERNS

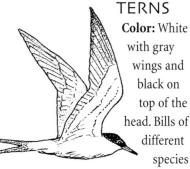

Color: White with gray wings and black on top of the head. Bills of different species are black, orange, or red.

Size: 9–21 inches (22.9–53.3 cm), depending on the type of tern.

Food: Small fish.

Notes: Look for terns flying above the coastline or nesting in marshy areas and on sandy beaches, especially along the calm Gulf Coast. (Never go near nesting birds. They may leave their eggs or babies unprotected if you scare them away.)

GREAT BLUE HERON

Color: Light tan when young, turns grayish blue as an adult.

Size: About 4 feet (1.2 m) tall. Spread of wings is 6 feet (1.8 m) tip to tip when flying.

Food: Fish and other aquatic animals.

Notes: Usually standing very still at the edge of marshy areas looking for fish and other food. Sometimes hard to spot even though it is a very big bird.

SANDPIPERS

Color: These birds are usually mottled brown, tan, and whitish.

Size: Dowitchers are about 11 inches (27.9 cm) long. Sanderlings are 8 inches (20.3 cm) long.

Food: Small clams and crabs found along the shore at the beach and in mudflats.

Notes: Dowitchers, sanderlings, and other sandpipers often walk along sandy beaches in the swash zone, the area on the sand that a wave has just washed over. They are looking for crabs and shellfish exposed or brought in by the ocean waves.

Sanderling

Dowitcher

SNOWY EGRET and GREAT EGRET

Color: White feathers, black legs. The snowy egret has a black bill and yellow feet. The great egret has a yellow bill.

Size: The snowy egret is up to 2 feet (0.6 m) tall. The great egret is about 3 feet (0.9 m) tall.

Food: Mostly fish and other aquatic animals.

Notes: Look for them walking in the shallow edges of estuaries and along seashores. As the snowy egret walks, it swishes its yellow feet in the water to stir up the animals it hunts for food.

Mammals and Fish

SCULPIN

Color: Yellowish or tan with brown lines and splotches; some may have red patches.
Size: About 3–4 in (7.6–10.2 cm) long.
Food: Small marine animals.
Notes: Look for these small fish in tide pools. They are common but blend in really well with the rocks and sand in the pool.

SEA LION

Color: Black when fur is wet; brownish when fur is dry.
Size: Up to 8 feet (2.4 m) long.
Food: Fish, shellfish, crabs, and other coastal marine animals.
Notes: Found on the Pacific Coast. Look for sea lions on rocks and beaches at the base of cliffs. You can hear the loud "barking" of groups of sea lions before you actually see them. The Steller sea lion of the Arctic and North Pacific rocky coastlines is yellowish brown and can grow up to 13 feet (3.9 m) long.

WHALES

Color: Gray whales are gray (of course) with possible lighter blotches. Humpback whales are black with white on their flippers and under their tail.
Size: Gray whales can be up to 46 feet (14.0 m) long. Humpback whales grow to about 53 feet (16.2 m) long.
Food: Krill (small, shrimplike animals) and small fish.
Notes: Both kinds of whales migrate north in spring and south in fall. Stand on bluffs or headlands along the coast to try and see them pass. Humpback whales sometimes breach, or leap, out of the water.

MANATEE

Color: Gray.
Size: Up to about 15 feet (4.6 m) long.
Food: Aquatic plants.
Notes: Found underwater in some of the bays and among the mangroves of the South Atlantic and Gulf Coasts. Because manatees often eat plants found near the surface of the water, they are sometimes injured by boats. Manatees became an endangered species in 1967.

RACCOON

Color: Grayish brown. A wide band of black across the eyes makes the raccoon look like it's wearing a mask. The tail is usually banded with black rings.
Size: About 3 feet (0.9 m) long.
Food: Amost everything from insects to other small animals to berries, etc.
Notes: Raccoons are nocturnal, so you may see them at night in salt marshes and along shallow shorelines of estuaries looking for food. If you don't see the raccoons, you may see their tracks, or footprints. Look on pages 10 and 44 for drawings of raccoon tracks.

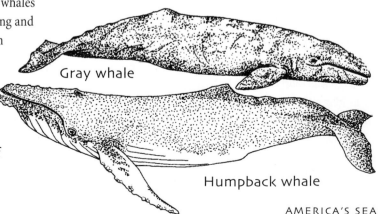

Gray whale

Humpback whale

Anemones, Worms, and Other Soft Creatures

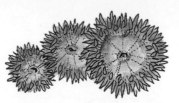

SEA CUCUMBER

Color: Orange, red, purplish, and brown are common colors.

Size: From 2–19 inches (5.1–48.3 cm) long.

Food: Tiny pieces of food floating in the water or on the sandy bottom. Sea cucumbers use their tentacles to grab food and then put the tentacles in their mouths to "lick" the food off.

Notes: Sea cucumbers are related to sea stars and sea urchins. All have tube feet, for example, and when the animal is underwater, you may be able to see those in lines down the side of the sea cucumber. Look for them in tide pools and under overhanging rocks during low tide. The orange-footed sea cucumber, which lives along the North Atlantic Coast, is one of the largest and easiest to find.

LUGWORM

Color: Black, very dark green, bloodred, and white are common colors.

Size: 6–12 inches (15.2–30.1 cm) long.

Food: Eats sand or mud to get the tiny pieces of food found there. Then it poops out the cleaned sand or mud from one of the openings to the burrow.

Notes: If you see what looks like thick round "noodles" of mud on the surface of a mudflat or sandy beach, those may be from a lugworm. These worms live in U-shaped burrows, hidden from view.

RIBBON WORM

Color: Light tan or cream-colored to reddish.

Size: From as short as 1 inch (2.5 cm) to as long as 20 feet (6.1 m)!

Food: Small marine animals.

Notes: Look for these worms under rocks during the day or swimming at night in mudflats. (If you move a rock, don't forget to put it back exactly as it was.)

ANEMONES

Color: Aggregating anemones are grayish or bluish green. Their tentacles have pinkish or bluish tips. Giant green anemones have green tentacles around a greenish or gray central disk.

Size: Aggregating anemones are about 3 inches (7.6 cm) wide. Giant green anemones are up to 10 inches (25.4 cm) wide.

Food: Tiny sea animals such as fish, shrimp, and crab are often paralyzed by an anemone's stinging tentacles. The tentacles then bring the food to the anemone's mouth in the center of its disk.

Notes: Look for large groups of aggregating anemones in tide pools on the Pacific Coast. If they're exposed to air during low tide, they will draw in their tentacles and close themselves up into what looks like grayish green blobs. The bright-green color and large size of the giant green anemones makes them easy to spot underwater in tide pools during low tide.

NUDIBRANCH or SEA SLUG

Color: Red, orange, yellow, blue, purple, brown, white, and gray. There's probably a nudibranch in just about any color you can think of.

Size: From about 1–6 inches (2.5–15.2 cm) long, depending upon species.

Food: Sponges, anemones, and barnacles are some of the marine animals eaten by different species of nudibranchs.

Notes: Many nudibranchs match the color of the food they eat. A red nudibranch may be found eating a red sponge, so you need to look carefully. There are two common groups of nudibranchs, one looks like flat snails without their shells and the other has what looks like rows of tentacles on their backs. During low tide, look in tide pools and under rocks to find them. (If you move a rock, remember to replace it just like it was before you moved it.)

Wildflowers

BEACH MORNING GLORY

Color: Pinkish flowers.

Size: Flowers and leaves stick up 2–8 inches (5.1–20.3 cm) from the sandy ground.

Notes: Found on dunes and bluffs at the ocean's edge.

ASTER

Color: Light purple or white with yellow centers.

Size: About 1–2 feet (0.3–0.6 m) tall. Flowers are about 1 inch (2.5 cm) across.

Notes: Salt marshes and coastal splash zones are good places to look for asters.

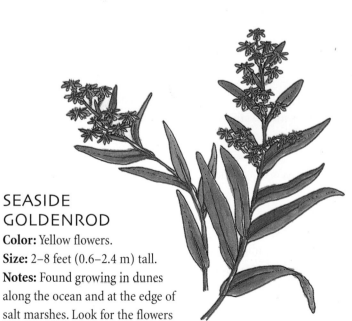

SEASIDE GOLDENROD

Color: Yellow flowers.

Size: 2–8 feet (0.6–2.4 m) tall.

Notes: Found growing in dunes along the ocean and at the edge of salt marshes. Look for the flowers from summer through fall.

BEACH PEA

Color: Purplish, pinkish, or reddish pink flowers.

Size: Stems grow along the ground, reaching 2–3 feet (0.6–0.9 m).

Notes: Found on sand dunes and ocean beaches.

Seaweeds, Kelp, and Other Algae

SEA LETTUCE

Color: Bright, light green.

Size: Up to 3 feet (0.9 m) long.

Notes: Sea lettuce looks wimpy out of water, like lettuce from the market that was partly frozen and left to thaw.

GIANT KELP

Color: Golden brown.

Size: Can grow to be more than 200 feet (61.0 m) long.

Notes: "Forests" of giant kelp provide homes and protection for many marine animals. The top of these forests float at the surface of the water along the Pacific coastline and can easily be seen from shore. Air-filled sections, called bladders, help keep the kelp floating.

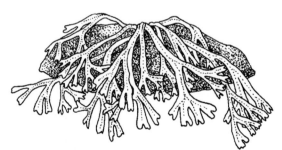

BULL KELP

Color: Olive green.

Size: Grows up to 100 feet (30.5 m) long.

Notes: Entire plants of bull kelp may be found washed up on beaches, especially after a storm.

ROCKWEED

Color: Brownish to olive green.

Size: The more common types of rockweed grow from 20 inches (50.8 cm) up to 4 feet (1.2 m) long.

Notes: Large areas of rocky shore may be covered by rockweed during mid-tide. Crabs, periwinkle snails, and other small animals often hide in the cool, wet, darkness underneath these brown algae. If you walk near rockweed that is exposed during low tide, be careful! It will be very slippery and rockweed may cover large openings between rocks where you could fall and hurt yourself. "Wrack" is another common name given to some rockweeds.

Grasses and Grasslike Plants

PICKLEWEED or GLASSWORT

Color: Green. In the fall, different species will either turn bright red, brown, or yellow.

Size: Stems grow up to about 20 inches (50.8 cm) tall.

Notes: The plant is called pickleweed along the Pacific Coast and glasswort along the Atlantic Coast. The succulent stems hold a lot of water and help the plant stay alive in the salty or brackish water of ocean beaches, salt marshes, and tidal flats.

SEA OATS

Color: Green leaves, green or tan stems. Tan seeds at top of stems.

Size: The leaves are 6–16 inches (15.2–40.6 cm) long. The entire plant can be up to 3–6 feet (0.9–1.8 m) tall.

Notes: This is a common plant on dunes of the Atlantic and Gulf Coasts. Roots and stems help keep the dune sand from blowing away.

EELGRASS

Color: Green leaves.

Size: Leaves are up to 4 feet (1.2 m) long.

Notes: Is the tide going out or coming in? Watch the leaves of this plant flow back and forth from the base as the tide comes in and out of estuaries and other shallow, brackish water along the shoreline. Crabs and other animals may be found among the long, tapelike leaves.

BEACH GRASS

Color: Green leaves, tan to light-green stems.

Size: Commonly 2–4 feet (0.6–1.2 m) tall.

Notes: Found on sand dunes, especially common along the Atlantic coastline. Beach grass stems and roots help hold the dune sand together so it doesn't blow away.

SALT GRASS

Color: Green leaves, green or tan stems.

Size: Usually 16 inches (40.6 cm) or less.

Notes: Found in salt marshes and other brackish areas.

Animal Tracks and Signs

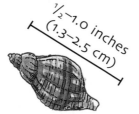

Moon snail

1–5 inches
(2.5–12.7 cm)

Razor clam with hole

2–5 inches (5.1–12.7 cm)

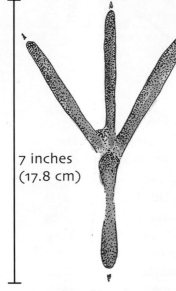

7 inches
(17.8 cm)

Great blue heron

1–5 inches
(2.5–12.7 cm)

Oyster with hole

As you walk along a wet, sandy beach or estuary during low tide, look at the empty shells that lay on the beach. Do any of them have tiny round holes near the hinge where the two shells come together? That's a **sign** that moon snails may have drilled through the shell and eaten the animal that lived inside. If the holes are in oyster, mussel, or barnacle shells, then the holes were probably made by oyster drill snails.

Sandy beaches and estuaries are excellent spots to find the **tracks**, or footprints, of gulls, great blue herons, and other animals that hunt or live there. You might even see tracks of raccoons, which don't live at the seashore but may come to look for food.

Another sign of animals along the shore are holes in the wet sand or mud. Some of them are made by clams or ghost shrimp living below the surface. And holes at or above the high-tide line may be the homes of nocturnal ghost crabs. Look for tracks leading into and out of these holes.

See how many animal tracks and signs you can find when you visit the seashore.

½–1.0 inches
(1.3–2.5 cm)

Oyster drill

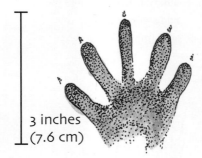

3 inches
(7.6 cm)

Raccoon

3 inches
(7.6 cm)

Gull

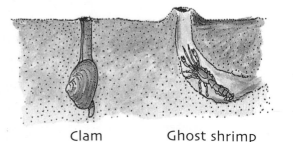

Clam   Ghost shrimp

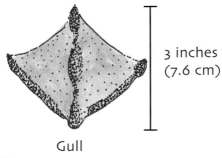

Ghost crab

Dowitcher (*Limnodromus* spp.) 3, 17, 23, 38

Dune grass (*Leymus mollis*) 24, 27, 28

Dusty miller (*Artemisia stelleriana*) 16

Eelgrass (*Zostera marina*) 8, 13, 24, 31, 33, 43, back cover

Egret (different genera) 5, 9, 17, 21, 24, 25, 38, back cover

Feather boa kelp (*Egregia menziesii*) 25

Fiddler crab (*Uca* spp.) 1, 3, 8, 15

Frilled anemone (*Metridium senile*) 32

Ghost crab (*Ocypode quadrata*) 9, 14, 44

Ghost shrimp (*Callianassa californiensis*) 27, 44

Giant Atlantic cockle (*Dinocardium robustum*) 35

Giant green anemone (*Anthopleura xanthogrammica*) front cover, 25, 27, 29, 40

Giant hermit crab (*Petrochirus diogenes*) 36

Giant kelp (*Macrocystis pyrifera*) 23, 24, 25, 42

Giant keyhole limpet (*Megathura crenulata*) 37

Giant Pacific chiton (*Cryptochiton stelleri*) 37

Glasswort (*Salicornia* spp.) 2, 9, 17, 20, 24, 43, 48

Glaucous gull (*Larus hyperboreus*) 32

Goose barnacle (*Pollicipes polymerus*) 25, 28, 34

Gray whale (*Eschrichtius robustus*) 28, 39

Great black-backed gull (*Larus marinus*) 12, 16

Great blue heron (*Ardea herodias*) 1, 17, 20, 23, 24, 26, 28, 38, 44, back cover

Great egret (*Casmerodius albus*) 17, 21, 24, 38

Green crab (*Carcinus maenas*) 12

Green sea urchin (*Strongylocentrotus droebachiensis*) 12, 29, 32, 37

Grunion (*Leuresthes tenuis*) 22

Gull (*Larus* spp.) front cover, 12, 9, 13, 16, 17, 20, 21, 22, 34, 44

Gumboot chiton (*Cryptochiton stelleri*) 28, 37

Gumweed (*Grindelia integrifolia*) 29

Harbor porpoise (*Phocoena phocoena*) 13

Harbor seal (*Phoca vitulina*) front cover, 13, 25, 27, 28, 35

Hermit crab (different genera) 13, 16, 21, 25, 28, 32, 34, 36

Herring gull (*Larus argentatus*) front cover, 12, 16, 21, 34

Horseshoe crab (*Limulus polyphemus*) 13, 15, 17

Humpback whale (*Megaptera novaeangliae*) 13, 39

Innkeeper worm (*Urechis caupo*) 23

Irish moss (*Chondrus crispus*) 5, 8, 11

Jaeger (*Stercorarius* spp.) 32

Kelp fly (different genera) 23

Keyhole limpet (different genera) 23, 24

Kittiwake (*Rissa tridactyla*) 31, 32

Knobbed whelk (*Busycon carica*) 16

Knotted wrack (*Ascophyllum nodosum*) 12

Laughing gull (*Larus atricilla*) 17, 20, 34

Leaf barnacle (*Pollicipes polymerus*) 34

Least tern (*Sterna antillarum*) 20

Lightning whelk (*Busycon contrarium*) 21

Limpet (different genera) 8, 12, 24, 28, 32, 37

Lined shore crab (*Pachygrapsus crassipes*) 24, 29

Lobster (*Homarus americanus*) 10

Loggerhead sea turtle (*Caretta caretta*) 18

Lugworm (*Arenicola* spp.) 40

Manatee (*Trichechus manatus*) 39

Mangrove (different genera) 7, 15, 21, back cover

Marsh periwinkle (*Littorina irrorata*) 35

Marsh rosemary (*Limonium californicum*) 24

Mermaid's purse 11, 21

Mole crab (*Emerita* spp.) 9, 36

Moon jelly (*Aurelia labiata*) 19

Moon snail (*Lunataria* spp. and other genera) front cover, 11, 13, 16, 32, 44

Mosquito (different genera) 31, 36

Mossy chiton (*Mopalia muscosa*) 25

Mottled seastar (*Evasterias troschelii*) 32

Murre (*Uria lomvia*) 9, 27, 31, 32

Mussels (*Mytilus* spp.) front cover, 8, 12, 17, 25, 28, 32, 35, 37

Needlerush (*Juncus* spp.) 17, 19, 20

Northern rock barnacles (*Balanus balanoides*) 34

Northern sea star (*Asterias vulgaris*) 12

Nudibranch (different genera) 32, 40

Ochre sea star (*Pisaster ochraceus*) front cover, 23, 25, 29, 37

Orange-footed sea cucumber (*Cucmaria frondosa*) 12

Orange-tipped nudibranch (*Triopha catalinae*) 32

Osprey (*Pandion haliaetus*) 13, 17, 21, 28

Owl limpet (*Lottia gigantea*) 24, 37

Oyster drill (*Urosalpinx cinerea*) 44

Oysters (*Crassostrea virginica*) 1, 3, 5, 15, 17, 44, back cover

Pea crab (*Scleroplax granulata*) 23

Pen shell (*Atrina* spp.) front cover

Periwinkle snail (*Littorina* and other genera) 7, 19, 35, 42

Phalarope (*Phalaropus fulicaris*) 33

Pickleweed (*Salicornia* spp.) 2, 9, 17, 20, 23, 24, 27, 43, 48

Plate limpet (*Notoacmaea* spp.) 12, 32

Polar bear (*Ursus maritimus*) 33

Portuguese man-of-war (*Physalia physalis*) 19, 20

Puffin (*Fratercula* spp.) 8, 9, 30

Purple sea urchin (*Strongylocentrotus purpuratus*) front cover, 25, 28, 37

Purple shore crab (*Hemigrapsus nudus*) 25, 29

Quahog (*Mercenaria mercenaria*) 16, 35

Raccoon (*Procyon lotor*) 10, 13, 17, 20, 39, 44, back cover

Railroad vine (*Ipomoea brasiliensis*) 20

Razor clam (different genera) 44

Red mangrove (*Rhizophora mangle*) 7, 15, 21, back cover

Red ribbon worm (*Tubulanus polymorphus*) 28

Red sea urchin (*Stronglocentrotus franciscanus*) 25, 28, 37

Red-throated loon (*Gavia stellata*) 33

Ribbon worm (different genera) 28, 40
Ringed seal (*Phoca hispida*) 31
Rock crab (*Cancer irroratus*) 12, 36, back cover
Rockweed (*Fucus spp.*) front cover, 5, 8, 11, 12, 25, 29, 42
Rough limpet (different genera) 24
Rough periwinkle (*Littorina saxatilis*) 12, 35
Rove beetle (*Thinopinus pictus*) 23
Royal tern (*Sterna maxima*) 21
Salt grass (*Distichlis spicata*) 9, 17, 27, 43
Salt hay (*Spartina patens*) 13
Salt marsh bulrush (*Scirpus robustus*) 17
Salt marsh dodder (*Cuscuta salina*) 28
Salt marsh mosquitoes (*Aedes* spp.) 36
Saltwort (*Batis maritima*) 23
Sand crabs (*Emerita* spp.) 36
Sand hoppers (different genera) 36
Sanderling (*Calidris alba*) 16, 21, 23, 38
Sandpiper (different genera) 18, 38
Sargassum weed (*Sargassum* spp.) 21
Scallop (different genera) front cover
Sculpin (different genera) 25, 28, 39
Sea anemones (different genera) front cover, 8, 25, 27, 29, 32, 40
Sea cucumber (different genera) 12, 40
Sea lettuce (*Ulva* spp.) 5, 17, 25, 42
Sea lion (different genera) 8, 27, 39
Sea nettles (*Chrysaora* spp.) 19
Sea oats (*Uniola paniculata*) 9, 15, 16, 20, 43, back cover

Sea otter (*Enhydra lutris*) 26
Sea oxeye daisy (*Borrichia arborescens*) 17
Sea palm (*Postelsia palmaeformis*) 27, 29
Sea purslane (*Sesuvium portulacastrum*) 17, 20
Sea rocket (*Cakile edentula*) 16
Sea slug (different genera) 40
Sea stars (different genera) front cover, 12, 23, 25, 27, 29, 32, 37, 40
Sea turtles (different genera) 18
Sea urchin (different genera) front cover, 8, 12, 25, 28, 29, 32, 37, 40
Sea-beach sandwort (*Honckenya peploides*) 33
Seals (different genera) 8
Seashore chamomile (*Tripleurospermum maritimum*) 33
Seashore lupine (*Lupinus littoralis*) 28
Seaside arrowgrass (*Triglochin maritimum*) 27, 33
Seaside bluebell (*Mertensia maritima*) 33
Seaside daisy (*Erigeron glaucus*) 29
Seaside goldenrod (*Solidago sempervirens*) front cover, 41
Seaside sparrow (*Ammodramus maritimus*) 19
Shadbush (*Amelanchier* spp.) 11
Shore pine (*Pinus contorta*) 28
Shrimp (different genera) 9
Silverweed (*Potentilla anserina*) 25
Sitka spruce (*Picea sitchensis*) 27, 29

Slipper shell (*Crepidula* spp.) front cover
Smooth sunstar (*Solaster endeca*) 12
Snowy egret (*Egretta thula*) 17, 21, 25, 38, back cover
Snowy plover (*Charadrius alexandrinus*) 21
Spider crab (*Libinia* spp.) 20
Sponge (different genera) 28, 40
Spotted seal (*Phoca larga*) 33
Steller sea lion (*Eumetopias jubatus*) 28, 39
Stingray (*Dasyatis americana*) 21
Sunburst lichen (*Xanthoria* spp.) 11, 13
Sunflower star (*Pycnopodia helianthoides*) 27, 29
Sunstar (*Crossaster paposus*) 32
Surf grass (*Phyllospadix* spp.) 25, 29
Terns (*Sterna* spp.) 9, 13, 19, 20, 25, 31, 33, 38, back cover
Thatched barnacle (*Semibalanus cariosus*) 28
Turkish towel (*Chondracanthus corymbiferus*) 25, 29
Verrucaria lichens (*Verrucaria* spp.) 13
Wavy turban snail (*Astraea undosa*) 24
Western gull (*Larus occidentalis*) 24, 28
Whales (different genera) 13, 28, 31, 32, 33, 39
White ibis (*Eudocimus albus*) 21
Willet (*Catoptrophorus semipalmatus*) 17, 23
Winterberry (*Ilex verticillata*) 11, 13
Wrack (different genera) 42
Yellowlegs (*Tringa* spp.) 13, 15, 17

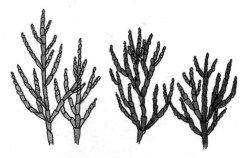

Pickleweed or Glasswort
(*Salicornia* spp.)